Cory

Martin

Miguel

Pearl

Mr. Whiskers

Ashley

Willie

Lupita

LARRY

What's the

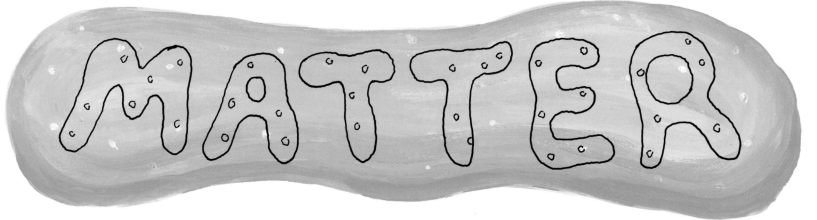

MATTER

in Mr. Whiskers' Room?

Michael Elsohn Ross

illustrated by **Paul Meisel**

CANDLEWICK PRESS
CAMBRIDGE, MASSACHUSETTS

To Samantha from Great Uncle Whiskers
M. E. R.

For Amy and Chris, and my friends at Candlewick
P. M.

Text copyright © 2004 by Michael Elsohn Ross
Illustrations copyright © 2004 by Paul Meisel

First edition 2004

Library of Congress Cataloging-in-Publication Data

Ross, Michael Elsohn, date.
What's the matter in Mr. Whiskers' Room? / Michael Elsohn Ross ;
illustrated by Paul Meisel. —1st ed.
p. cm.
ISBN 0-7636-1349-5
1. Science—Experiments—Juvenile literature.
[1. Science—Experiments. 2. Experiments.]
I. Meisel, Paul, ill. II. Title.
Q164.R69 2004
507'.8—dc22   2003069566

2 4 6 8 10 9 7 5 3 1

Printed in China

This book was typeset in Stempel Schneidler and Gill Sans.
The illustrations were done in ink and watercolor.
Colored pencil, gouache, and pastels were also used.

Candlewick Press
2067 Massachusetts Avenue
Cambridge, Massachusetts 02140

visit us at www.candlewick.com

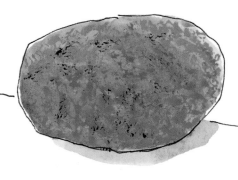

A NOTE TO BIG PEOPLE

Kids learn about science by exploring. In my class, I promote open-ended discovery. I watch and listen to the kids at play, and when I think they are ready to consider a big idea, I introduce one, such as "Matter takes up space." All people are born scientists. We are curious and naturally experiment. As adults we can nurture exploration in our children, but we need not meddle in their enthusiastic adventures (unless there is a matter of safety involved).

Mr. Whiskers

One hot Monday in early September, Martin arrived at school with a bellyache. But when he walked into the classroom, he almost forgot all about it.

Mr. Whiskers had a wild look in his eyes, the kind that said something fun was going to happen. There were science kits set up at tables and even outside in the schoolyard. Lots of kids had questions about the kits, but when Mr. Whiskers waved his silence wand, everyone quieted down.

"What's the matter with your stomach, Martin?" whispered Ashley.

"Matter? Did I hear someone say matter?" Mr. Whiskers asked. "That's exactly what we are going to explore today. Matter is stuff, and I have lots of stuff for you to play with."

All the kids wanted to see the stuff, but first Mr. Whiskers pointed out the rules for explorer time.

When he tooted the horn, everyone scattered. Some kids looked at the kits in the classroom, and some checked out the science stations in the schoolyard.

10

RULES

Start to play when you hear the horn.

Share with other people.

Change groups whenever you wish or when it's too crowded.

Be gentle with things and people.

Have fun.

Help put everything away when I beat the drum.

11

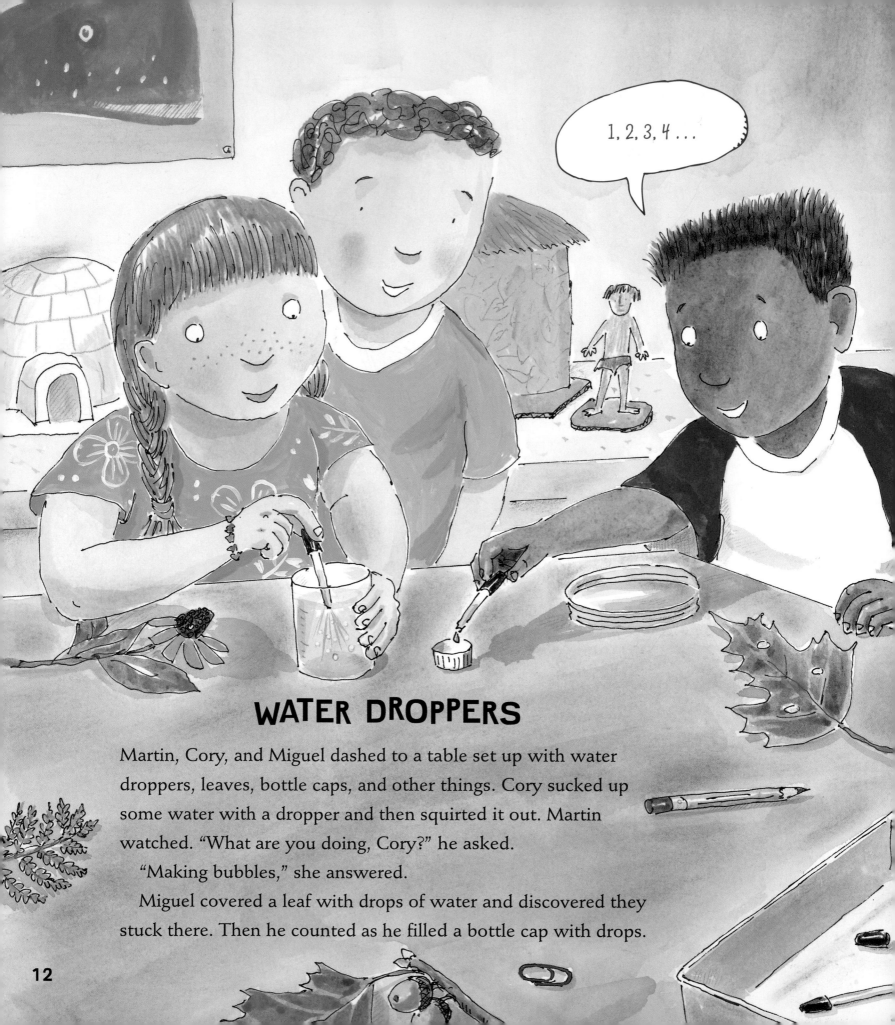

WATER DROPPERS

Martin, Cory, and Miguel dashed to a table set up with water droppers, leaves, bottle caps, and other things. Cory sucked up some water with a dropper and then squirted it out. Martin watched. "What are you doing, Cory?" he asked.

"Making bubbles," she answered.

Miguel covered a leaf with drops of water and discovered they stuck there. Then he counted as he filled a bottle cap with drops.

12

"Let's do something really fun," Cory announced. She pretended the dropper was a drippy nose. Willie cruised by and looked at Cory but didn't stay to play.

Miguel stuck drops to a pencil, a paper clip, his fingernail, and even to Mr. Whiskers' nose.

"Does water take up space?" Mr. Whiskers asked.

"Water fills up my dropper," said Martin.

Miguel replied, "Drops can fill up a bottle cap."

"Look! Bubbles take up space," Cory announced.

"Toys take up a lot of space in my room," Martin said. "Too much space, my mom says. Hey, maybe everything takes up space."

"That's the big idea," Mr. Whiskers told him. "All matter takes up space!"

I take up space at this table!

14

A BIG IDEA!

Everything around us is matter, and all matter takes up space.

Air takes up space in a balloon, and water takes up space in a bathtub. The bigger the object, the more space it takes up. Look around you. Can you see matter taking up space? Which things take up the most space?

Snot takes up space in your nose.

15

GLOOP

Martin saw Larry and Ashley over at a table with some interesting blue gloopy stuff. He got there just as Larry grabbed as much of the gloop as he could. "Mine, all mine!" Larry said.

"Larry, you're supposed to share," Ashley reminded him. "Now give some to Martin and me."

Larry frowned but gave a bit to each of the others.

Cory came over and took a chunk from Larry too.

"Hey, this feels like rubber," she said.

"It looks like taffy," said Martin.

"It stretches," said Ashley. "Maybe we can add all of ours together and make a snake."

I wish the stretchy snake was mine!

"Maybe we can make candy and eat it," added Martin. "Yum!"

"Martin," Mr. Whiskers called out just as Martin was about to taste some gloop. "Remember, we don't eat any matter during science class, no matter how good it looks."

Ashley said, "Look, Mr. Whiskers. It stretches!"

It's squishy and stretchy and bubbly.

A BIG IDEA!

We can find out about matter by using our senses.

For example, a carrot is matter, and it has a particular taste, smell, color, and shape. Carrots even make a crunchy, snappy sound when you bite into them. We can sense other things too. We can't see air, but we can feel it when the wind blows, and smell the scents that it carries.

"Hmmm," Mr. Whiskers said. "What else did you discover about gloop?"

"Its bubbles make a loud pop!" Cory cried out.

Martin whined, "It looks and smells good enough to eat."

"That's the big idea!" said Mr. Whiskers. "We can find out about matter by using our senses of touch, sight, hearing, and smell. We can also use our sense of taste, but not here, Martin!"

19

OOBLECK

"Hey, Pearl, what's that stuff?" called Cory as she sat down between Pearl and Miguel at another science station.

They had green slimy stuff dripping from their fingers and squashed between their palms.

"It's oobleck and it changes from hard to soft and back again," Pearl said.

It's slimy like squished bananas.

"It's like magic," Miguel said. "It's hard when it's in the dish, but it's drippy when you pick it up."

Martin and Lupita ambled over to the group.

Cory pretended she was sick and cried out, "I'm throwing up green gunk!"

"It's kind of like glue—maybe it would glue your mouth up," Martin said.

"Maybe I can glue my hands together," said Miguel.

It's green and icky!

Mr. Whiskers squeezed some oobleck and let it drip through his fingers. "Do you think this is a liquid, like milk, or a solid, like a cookie?" he asked Cory.

"Sometimes it drips, and sometimes it's solid," she answered.

"It's kind of like a milk shake and kind of like ice cream," added Martin.

A BIG IDEA!

Matter can come in different forms.

It can be a liquid, a solid, or a gas. Rocks, bones, and trees are solids. Water, lava, and blood are liquids. Helium, propane, and oxygen are gases. What forms of matter can you find around you? Can you locate any gases, liquids, or solids?

"It's hard, but it's gooey," said Pearl.

"I noticed that too," said Mr. Whiskers. "Matter can be a gas, a liquid, or a solid. The fun thing about oobleck is that it changes from a solid to a liquid, then back again."

23

ICE AND WATER

Cory wandered outdoors into the warm sunshine. She spied the
blocks of ice that Mrs. Sanchez, the classroom aide, was placing on
the blacktop for another science kit. Then Cory set to work inventing
an ice-melting machine with mirrors and tinfoil.

"What are you doing, Cory?" Ashley asked.

"I'm going to cook the ice," Cory replied.

Miguel came by and started to write on the blacktop with water
and a paintbrush.

"Do you think water will melt the ice?" Ashley asked Cory.

Cory thought for a minute, then said, "I know soda melts ice cubes."

"I sprayed some ice with water, and it melted the ice," Ashley reported.

"My name disappeared from the ground," Miguel added. "Maybe I invented disappearing ink."

Cory asked, "Do you think my ice-melting machine is working?"

When Mr. Whiskers walked by, Miguel called out, "Come and see the disappearing ink."

Mr. Whiskers examined the blacktop and then asked, "Where did the water ink go? Do you think the water changed to something else?"

"I saw steam," Miguel said.

I made ice into water.

"Cory's ice was solid," Ashley said. "But when it melted, it became liquid."

"Maybe the water changed to steam," Cory added. "It evaporated!"

"That's the big idea!" Mr. Whiskers exclaimed. "Matter can change form—from liquid to solid or gas. The ice changed to water, and the water changed to vapor."

A BIG IDEA!

Matter can change from one form to another.

For instance, ice is solid matter. When it melts, it becomes liquid water. Liquid water can evaporate and become water vapor or steam, which is a gas. Water vapor can condense and become liquid water again. Liquid water can then freeze and become ice. Can *you* make water change form? What other matter can you find that changes form?

ROCKS

Ashley went looking for Larry, and found him inside at a table covered with rocks, scales, magnifying lenses, cups of water, tiles, and other things.

She peered at a rock through a magnifying lens and saw sparkles. Larry scraped one rock against another and rubbed his finger over the scratches that he had made. Then he made scratches on other rocks.

Ashley put little rocks on one side of the scale. When she put a big rock on the other side, it sank down.

"Look," she said to Martin, who had wandered over. "This rock is heavier than three little ones."

"This little one looks like a pill," Martin said, and he almost swallowed it but remembered what Mr. Whiskers had said. He dropped it in the water, and it changed color.

Ashley ran over to Mr. Whiskers and pulled him to the table.

"I found the heavyweight rock," she told him.

"Do all rocks have weight?" Mr. Whiskers asked.

"Of course. I think everything has weight," said Ashley.

"If I ate something, I'd have more weight," said Martin.

"If you gave me all the rocks, I'd have a lot of weight," said Larry.

Mr. Whiskers said, "Yes, that's another big idea. All matter has weight!"

I think *my rock* is the heaviest.

A BIG IDEA!
All matter has weight.
The more dense an object is, the more it weighs. A pencil is more dense than a straw, so the pencil weighs more than the straw. A book is more dense than a dry sponge of the same size, so the sponge weighs less than the book. What things can you find that are really heavy? What can you find that is light?

31

WATER TUBS

Larry and Ashley wanted to try something new, so they went outside to do some tests at the water tubs.

"Wow, look at all this stuff!" exclaimed Larry. He grabbed as much as he could. He even tried to take some things that Lupita was using.

"Remember the rules, Larry. You have to share," said Ashley.

Lupita pretended she was giving a toy dinosaur a bath. Willie was hot from wandering all over the place and was cooling off as he poured water through funnels onto one of his hands.

Larry and Ashley found out that an empty bowl floated, but then it sank when they filled it with water. A cork floated, but Lupita's dinosaur sank.

"I wonder what else will float," Ashley said.

"Put the dinosaur in an empty bowl and see what happens," Larry suggested.

The dinosaur rode along inside the floating bowl as if it were in a boat. Willie put a rock in the water and that floated too!

34

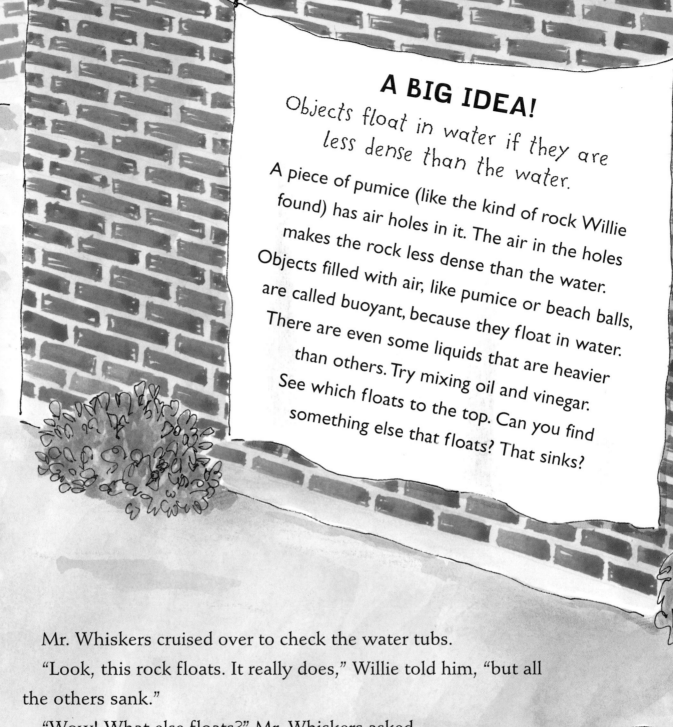

A BIG IDEA!

Objects float in water if they are less dense than the water.

A piece of pumice (like the kind of rock Willie found) has air holes in it. The air in the holes makes the rock less dense than the water. Objects filled with air, like pumice or beach balls, are called buoyant, because they float in water. There are even some liquids that are heavier than others. Try mixing oil and vinegar. See which floats to the top. Can you find something else that floats? That sinks?

Mr. Whiskers cruised over to check the water tubs.

"Look, this rock floats. It really does," Willie told him, "but all the others sank."

"Wow! What else floats?" Mr. Whiskers asked.

"Empty bowls float," replied Larry.

"Bowls full of water sink," added Ashley.

"Remember, the baby dinosaur sank," Lupita reminded them.

"I like to float sticks," said Ashley.

"So it looks like some matter sinks and some floats," said Mr. Whiskers. "Guess what? That's another big idea!"

SAND AND MUD PLAY

Looking for something messier to play with, Cory and Miguel went to the sandbox.

Ashley was there, making cookies from a special recipe of mud, sand, and leaves. Larry was about to take away some of her leaves, but she suggested, "Larry, let's make something together."

"Okay. Let's make a *giant* cookie," said Larry.

They mixed leaves and mud together and made a cookie, but when Larry poured water on it, it turned all mucky.

Larry and Ashley got busy testing new recipes for dirt cookies.
They added more dirt and more water, a little bit at a time.

"Let's make a pretend volcano with dirt," Cory said to Miguel.
"And then we can make some lava by filling the hole on the top of
the volcano with water."

"One, two, three, four, five." Miguel counted the cups of water as
he poured them into the hole. When the hole was full, a river of mud
oozed downhill.

When Mr. Whiskers was nearby, Larry told him, "The water drank up the dirt in our cookie and made it soggy."

"But then we put in some extra dirt, and it drank up the water and made it more solid again," said Ashley. "Look." And she rushed over to show Mr. Whiskers their cookie, but she tripped and it landed on his shoes.

"Oops. Sorry, Mr. Whiskers," apologized Ashley.

"It's only cookie dough," said Mr. Whiskers as he washed it off with water.

Do you like cookies, Mr. Whiskers?

"Watch this, Mr. Whiskers," Miguel called out as he poured water into the volcano to make more lava.

"It looks like the water dissolves the dirt when it makes your lava," observed Mr. Whiskers.

"Yeah," replied Miguel, "it sucks it up and carries it away."

"Wow!" said Mr. Whiskers. "It seems like some matter dissolves other matter. What do you know? That's another big idea."

A BIG IDEA!

Some matter dissolves other matter.

Sugar mixes with water to make sugar water.

Salt mixes with water to make salt water.

Sand doesn't dissolve in water but sinks to the bottom. Dirt will dissolve in water, but after a while it will also sink.

Only the tiniest particles of dirt will stay in the water, giving it a dirty color.

When a substance dissolves in water, the new substance is called a solution. Can you make some solutions with water and other matter?

The things we know about
matter:

When Mr. Whiskers beat the drum, the kids started putting things away. Soon all the kits were on the carts, and the children were sitting on the floor in front of Mr. Whiskers.

He waved his silence wand and then announced, "Raise your hand if you want to tell the class what you learned about matter."

All the kids raised their hands, and Mr. Whiskers wrote down all the things that they had to say about matter.

"So, what you're telling me," Mr. Whiskers said, "is that matter is everywhere and everything is matter. You are matter. I am matter. Everything from Popsicles to planets is matter!

"I bet you can discover all sorts of wild things about the matter in your house and out in your neighborhood too. Just don't forget to tell the rest of us about them, okay?"

The science fun was over for the day, but all the kids knew that Mr. Whiskers would bring in more strange and wonderful things to explore.

MR. WHISKERS' KIT AND CABOODLE

Do you want to do some exploring at home or in school? Here are some recipes to help you! Each tells you what materials you'll need and even sometimes where you can get them. You can store all the materials in plastic washtubs.

Have a wild time,

Mr. Whiskers

P.S. A note to adults: Kids will use the kit materials in many ways. As you listen to them and watch them, you'll learn about their discoveries.

WATER DROPPERS, pages 12–15

Use plastic droppers from old medicine bottles (make sure they are washed well) or buy some droppers. (See page 45 for ordering information.) Collect some toys, and stuff like twigs, stones, or leaves to drip water on. Use food coloring to make colored water.

GLOOP, pages 16–19

It's best to play with gloop on a sheet of plastic or on an old tablecloth. Put it away in a closed container when you are done or it will dry and get hard.

1. In a large bowl, add 1 cup of water to 2 cups of white glue.
2. Fill three cups each with 1/3 cup of warm water.
3. Stir a teaspoon of borax into each cup of warm water.
4. Mix one of the cups of borax water into the glue mixture, and then add the others, one at a time. The mix will get very gloopy, but stir until all the water is mixed in.
5. Store in a plastic container with a lid.

Provide small toys, marbles, string, cups, and cookie cutters for use with the gloop.

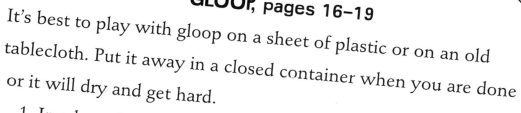

OOBLECK, pages 20–23

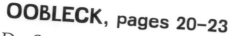

(Remember Dr. Seuss's *Bartholomew and the Oobleck?*)
Play with this at a picnic table outside or inside on a washable tablecloth. Have a bucket of water handy to rinse off your hands when you finish playing.

Mix 7 tablespoons of cornstarch with 4 tablespoons of water a little at a time until you get a mixture that is solid when still but melts into a liquid when held. Stir in a little green paint or food coloring. Store it in a plastic container with a lid.

ICE AND WATER, pages 24–27

This is fun to play outside on the sidewalk, blacktop, or on the patio floor.

Make some blocks of ice by freezing water in large plastic containers or gallon milk cartons. You can use old window-washer spray bottles or buy new ones at the store. Watercolor brushes or old paintbrushes work well for painting with water.

ROCKS, pages 28–31

Get pumice from your local volcano (or see page 45 for ordering information) and collect rocks from your neighborhood. Then use the things in this list to explore with: balance scale, magnifying lenses, unglazed tile, tub of water, paintbrushes.

WATER TUBS, pages 32–35

You can play with water outside in the yard or in the bathtub, where it won't matter if you get wet.

Fill a large bucket or tub with water and then use the stuff in this list to play with: funnels, corks, pebbles, pieces of pumice, balls, brushes, plastic bottles and containers, sponges, turkey basters, small toys, and sponges. At the hardware store get some two- to three-foot long pieces of acrylic tubing and some PVC pipe fittings and pipe. (They can cut the pipe into two-foot pieces for you there.)

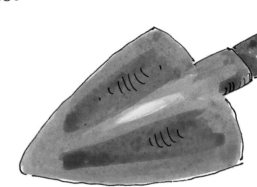

SAND AND MUD PLAY, pages 36–39

Set these materials up in a sandbox or other good digging spot: food containers of various sizes, cookie cutters and molds, large horseshoe magnet, kitchen strainers, trowels or small sand shovels, spoons or forks.

Where to order kit materials:

NASCO: Balance scales, water droppers (pipettes), magnets. 1-800-558-9595, www.homeschool-nasco.com

Carolina Biological Supply Co. 1-800-334-5551, www.carolina.com

Discount School Supply 1-800-334-2014, www.kaplanco.com